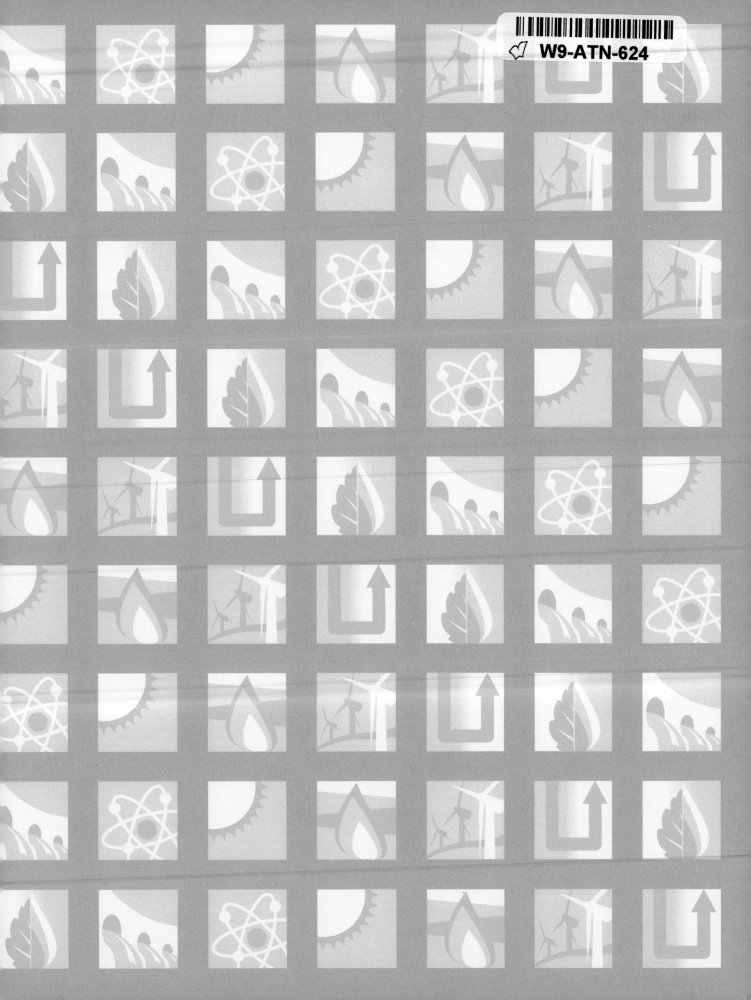

ENERGY SOURCES

Facts · Issues · The Future

# FOSSIL FUELS

## NEIL MORRIS

A+

**Smart Apple Media**

Published by Smart Apple Media
2140 Howard Drive West
North Mankato, MN 56003
Designed by Guy Callaby
Edited by Mary-Jane Wilkins
Picture research by Su Alexander

Photograph acknowledgements
Title page & page 4 Craig Aurness/Corbis; 5 David Butow/Corbis Saba;
6 Charles Mauzy/Corbis; 7t Chinch Gryniewicz; Ecoscene/Corbis, b Tim
Wright/Corbis; 8 Corbis; 9 Hulton-Deutsch Collection/Corbis; 10 Colin
Garratt; Milepost 92 1/2/Corbis; 11 Schenectady Museum; Hall of Electrical
History Foundation/Corbis; 12 Dean Conger/Corbis; 13t Roger Ressmeyer/
Corbis, b Reinhard Krause/Reuters/Corbis; 14 Claro Cortes IV/Reuters/Corbis;
15 Paul Stuart; Eye Ubiquitous/Corbis; 16 Bettmann/Corbis; 17t Bettmann/
Corbis, b Roger Wood/Corbis; 18 Shepard Sherbell/Corbis Saba; 19t Michael
St. Maur Sheil/Corbis, b Reuters/Corbis; 20 Richard Klune/Corbis; 21 Pitchal
Frederic/Corbis Sygma; 22 Scott T. Smith/Corbis; 23 Sergio Dorantes/Corbis;
24 Charles E. Rotkin/Corbis; 25 Georgina Bowater/Corbis; 26 Bossu Regis/
Corbis Sygma; 27 (background) Randy Faris/Corbis, (forefront) Kennard
Ward/Corbis; 28 Pitchal Frederic/Corbis Sygma; 29t James L. Amos/Corbis,
b Ian Harwood; Ecoscene/Corbis; Front cover Lowell Georgia/Corbis

Printed in China

Library of Congress Cataloging-in-Publication Data

Morris, Neil, 1946-
Fossil fuels / by Neil Morris.
p. cm. — (Energy sources)
Includes index.
ISNB-13: 978-1-58340-905-3
1. Fossil fuels—Juvenile literature. I. Title. II. Series.

TP318.3.M67 2006
553.2—dc22          2005046784

First Edition

9 8 7 6 5 4 3 2 1

# Contents

# Energy from underground

The world's fossil fuels—coal, oil, and natural gas—are some of our most valuable sources of energy. They are called fossil fuels because all three substances come from the fossilized remains of prehistoric plants and animals.

## NONRENEWABLE RESOURCES

People have been burning coal, oil, and gas for hundreds of years. Today, we are using up these resources at a faster rate than ever before. This creates a major problem, because fossil fuels take many thousands—or even millions—of years to form underground. They are nonrenewable resources, which means that we will run out of them at some point in the future. Experts believe that the world's coal may run out in about 200 years. Underground reserves of oil and gas may last for only 60 years if we continue to mine and use them at the same rate as we do now.

*A miner drills coal from the wall of an underground mine.*

We use these fuels to provide the power to work machines, as well as to light and heat our homes, offices, and factories. The term energy comes from the Greek word *energos*, meaning active or working. Energy sources help other things become active and do work, such as lifting or moving objects. For example, all three fossil fuels can be used to make electricity. So when you switch on an electric light in your home, the energy to make it work might have come from a power station that is fired by burning coal, oil, or gas.

## Running on oil

Oil is used to power the world's cars, trains, ships, and planes. To make this possible, the crude oil that we get from beneath the ground is refined, or processed, into gasoline for cars, diesel oil for trains and ships, and jet fuel for planes. These fuels are so popular that we produce and use more than 75 million barrels of oil every day (and every barrel contains about 42 gallons, or 159 l). The lives of many people in today's world have become dependent on oil.

*Some of these drivers probably get stuck in a traffic jam every day on their way to work. Their cars burn expensive gas, and their exhaust fumes pollute the air.*

# All kinds of coal

If you pick up a lump of coal, you will hold in your hands the remains of plants that lived on Earth hundreds of millions of years ago. That was long before the first dinosaurs or humans appeared on the planet.

Most coal began to form during a time we call the Carboniferous Period, or the age of coal forests. During this period, which lasted from about 360 to 286 million years ago, swampy forests of giant ferns covered the land. When the plants died, they did not completely decay but were buried under a layer of mud. As more plants died, they piled up in further layers. Eventually, the pressure of these layers turned the vegetation below into a spongy mass called peat. This is the first stage in the formation of coal, and dried peat can also be burned as fuel.

*Ferns and moss grow beside fallen trees in a forest today. Prehistoric forests may have looked a bit like this, with giant ferns instead of woody trees.*

## Brown and soft coals

Over a long period of time, weight and pressure from layers above turned peat into a soft, crumbly kind of coal. We call this lignite (from the Latin for wood), and it is also known as brown coal. The next layer, deeper down beneath the lignite, is made up of bituminous coal (from bitumen, a kind of tarry pitch). This is often called soft coal, though it is much harder than lignite or peat. Bituminous is the most common kind of coal, and many factories burn it to provide heat and power.

## Black diamonds

At the deepest level beneath the surface, pressure turned bituminous coal into a glossy black coal called anthracite (from the Greek for coal). This is known as hard coal. It is the least plentiful kind, but it burns more slowly and gives off less smoke than other coals. Years ago, in the coal-mining region of eastern Pennsylvania, lumps of anthracite were valued so highly that they were known as black diamonds.

*An excavating machine digs lignite at this surface mine in Germany. Lignite is the youngest form of coal. Some of it may have formed during the past million years.*

*Anthracite is often mined in large chunks and then broken down into smaller lumps such as these. This hard coal is about 98 percent carbon, the element that also forms diamonds. Most brown lignite contains less than a third the amount of carbon.*

# History of coal

People have been burning coal for thousands of years. Archaeologists have found evidence of people burning it in northern Europe up to 4,000 years ago.

Coal was burned to smelt copper in ancient China, and it was a popular fuel with the ancient Greeks and Romans. By A.D. 1200, it was burned in fires on both sides of the Atlantic.

*Many children and young people were sent down mines to dig coal in past centuries. These young miners worked in Pennsylvania in 1911.*

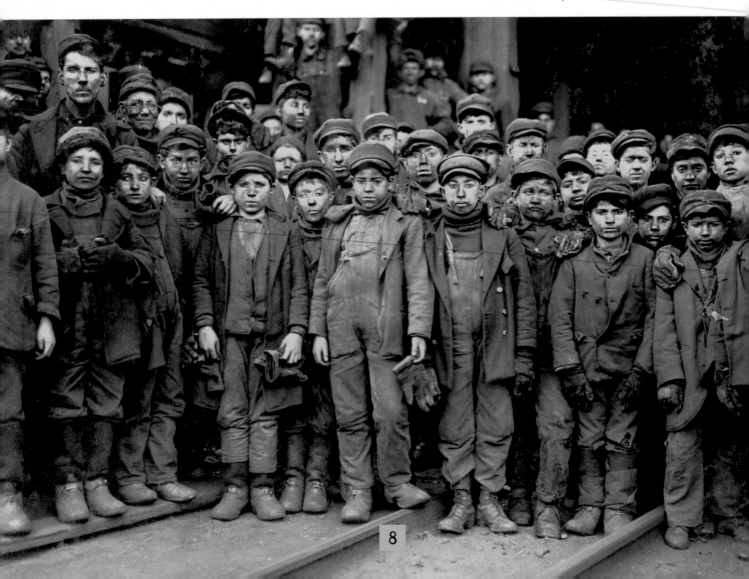

In North America, the Hopi people scraped coal from dry valleys and used it to fuel kilns and bake pottery. In 13th-century Britain, people heated their homes by burning coal that came mostly from the northeast coast of Northumberland. They called this sea coal, and it made a smokier and sootier fire than wood. A few centuries later, when wood became scarce because so many British trees had been cut down, more coal was burned again.

## Coke and iron

People discovered that if they heated bituminous coal in an airtight oven, it gave off gases and tar rather than burning. The coal then turned into a substance called coke, which gives off great heat but little smoke when it burns.

In 1709, an English iron-maker named Abraham Darby converted a furnace to burn coke instead of charcoal, which comes from wood. The new furnace was much more effective for smelting iron and made it easier and cheaper to produce the metal. Today, coke is still used in factories that make iron and steel.

## Household heating

Many houses had coal fires until around the middle of the 20th century. People had to buy coal from a merchant. It was delivered to the door by a coalman and stored in a coalbin. Coal fires were hard work because they had to be constantly tended, and they left behind piles of ashes, which had to be cleared away. The coal also gave off a lot of smoke, which polluted the air and in some cities caused smog (shortened from smoke fog). During the 1950s, cities such as London introduced smokeless zones, where only fuels similar to coke could be burned.

*This old photograph shows a coalman blowing up a tire on his horse-drawn cart. His coal is stored in large sacks.*

 # Steam power

About 2,000 years ago, a Greek mathematician, Hero of Alexandria, invented a machine that was powered by steam. The machine was probably not very practical, but during the 18th century, scientists and engineers in Britain began to realize that steam could be used to power machines.

*The fireman of a steam locomotive shovels coal into the firebox. This heats water in a boiler to keep up a steady supply of steam and push pistons that turn the wheels.*

This knowledge brought about the Industrial Revolution, when factories were built so that textiles and other goods could be mass-produced. This revolution was powered by steam, produced by burning coal to heat water. The burning coal heated water until it turned into steam, which pushed a piston that turned a wheel. During the 18th century, Britain mined vast amounts of coal, and the supply seemed endless. Today, coal is still used to produce steam in power stations all around the world.

## The coming of the railroad

At the beginning of the 19th century, engineers started building the first steam locomotives. At first they were used to pull wagons in ironworks and other factories. But people saw the potential for transportation, and in 1825, a locomotive built by George Stephenson pulled the world's first public steam train.

The locomotives carried their own coal and water in a tender behind the main engine. They worked well and soon became a worldwide success. By 1869, there were railroad tracks across North America, and coal-fired locomotives ran the railways until the middle of the 20th century. In the late 1940s, diesel locomotives (using a form of oil) began to replace steam engines.

## First power station

The world's first power station opened in 1882 in New York. The Pearl Street plant used huge amounts of coal to power steam engines and generate electricity. This first plant could provide power for only a small section of New York's Manhattan district, but new developments were on the way. One was the introduction of efficient steam turbines in 1895 by American inventor Charles Curtis. Later versions of these turbines are still used in power stations that run on fossil fuels today.

*An early Curtis steam turbine. Inside the machine, steam turned a set of blades attached to a wheel.*

# Coal mining

**S**ome seams, or layers, of coal are close to the earth's surface. Layers of rock and soil, which miners call the overburden, cover the coal.

In strip mines, workers first use drills and explosives to break up the overburden. They then use power shovels to lift and remove the rubble, so the coal can be dug up. Large coal-digging machines scoop up the coal and load it onto trucks, which take it out of the mine.

If the land above a coal seam is hilly, machines cut wide ledges into the hillside. But if the coal seams are deeper underground, the machines dig vertical shafts from the surface. They then dig horizontal tunnels to the seams. In most underground mines, mechanical cutters gouge out the coal, and conveyor belts carry it to a main shaft.

*You can see the ledges that have been cut in this strip mine in Mongolia. Cargo trains carry mined coal to the nearest towns and cities.*

After the spinning teeth of a longwall shearer have bitten into the seam, coal is carried away on a conveyor belt.

## Modern methods

Early miners used picks and shovels to dig coal from deep beneath the earth. Drills gradually replaced these manual tools. In recent years, new machines have taken over some of the work. Underground mines with seams of coal hundreds of feet long have powerful longwall shearers, or cutting machines. These travel along the seam and cut the coal. Steel supports hold up the roof above the machine and the miners operating it. The roof is then allowed to collapse behind the machine as it moves forward. The longwall method is quick and efficient.

A coal truck loads up at Fuxin in China. The Sunjiawan mine employs 3,100 people and produces 1.7 millions tons (1.5 million t) of coal a year.

# Coal around the world

Coal is a worldwide resource. All of the world's continents have coal, and there are coal deposits beneath the oceans, too. Asia produces the most coal, followed by Europe and North America.

More than 60 countries mine coal, and the leading producers are China and the United States. These two countries together extract half of the coal mined in the world every year. The amount of coal mined in China has grown, and today the Chinese mine more than twice as much as 20 years ago.

China also produces more than three-quarters of the world's anthracite (the oldest and highest-quality coal). Germany produces the most lignite (brown coal), followed by Russia. Coal mining continues to grow in some regions but is dwindling in others.

*A barge tows a large cargo of coal along China's Grand Canal. Most coal is mined in the northeast of the country.*

## Coal from Australia

Coal was discovered in Australia in 1791, and 10 years later, a ship carried its first cargo of coal from New South Wales to India. During the 19th and 20th centuries, the Australian coal industry continued to grow. By 1982, Australia was mining more coal than Britain, and it went on exporting large amounts. The Australians are still finding new deposits and opening new mines. Nearly three-quarters are strip mines, such as the Burton Mine in Queensland, which started producing coal in 1996. The next year, the Crinum underground mine began production in the same region, using the longwall method (see page 13).

*This mine in South Wales no longer produces coal but has become a National Mining Museum. The tall building is a winding house, which holds the cables that once lowered miners down the shaft.*

(see page 13)

## CHANGING WAY OF LIFE

During the late 17th century, Britain produced more than three-quarters of the world's coal. Today, it produces less than one per cent, and the amount drops every year as more mines close. There are only nine working coal mines left in Britain, which imports more coal from other countries than it mines. Much of the country's electricity is now produced by gas-fired power stations. In areas such as South Wales, whole towns and communities have changed their way of life because they grew up around coal mines that are no longer operating.

# History of gas and oil

The ancient Chinese discovered natural gas when they dug wells for underground brine (salty water) more than 2,000 years ago. They probably burned the gas to boil the brine and recover the salt.

In other parts of the ancient world, people found and lit gas that sprang from cracks in the ground. Near the Caspian Sea, worshipers visited temples with "eternal fires" of burning gas. At the same time, ancient peoples used a sticky form of oil, called pitch or tar, to waterproof their boats.

During the 19th century, people started digging pits to bring oil up to the surface from natural deposits. Then, in 1859, a retired railway conductor named Edwin Drake used a steam-driven machine to drill for oil in Pennsylvania. His success—the first real oil well—encouraged others to drill for "black gold" in other parts of the world.

*Edwin Drake's success created a rush of other oil prospectors in Pennsylvania. This was similar to the gold rush in California 10 years earlier. Wells soon sprang up wherever oil was found.*

16

## Lighting homes and streets

In the 17th century, a Belgian chemist discovered that he could make gas by heating coal. Later, a British engineer found a way to light his home by burning coal gas. The technology developed quickly, and in 1807, the first gaslights appeared in London streets. Fourteen years later, engineers in the U.S. piped natural gas from a well through hollowed-out logs and used it for lighting. Gaslights were very popular in homes and streets, and soon many different gas companies sprang up.

## Oil beneath the desert

A French geologist first discovered oil beneath the Persian Desert (in present-day Iran) in 1890. After a similar discovery was made in 1936 on the other side of the Persian Gulf, in Saudi Arabia, the oil industry grew throughout the Middle East. In 1960, four Middle Eastern countries—Iran, Iraq, Kuwait and Saudi Arabia—joined with Venezuela to form an organization that controlled the price of the oil they sold to oil companies around the world. Today, OPEC (the Organization of Petroleum Exporting Countries) has 11 member countries, which together produce nearly half of the world's oil.

*Gaslights had to be lit individually, and most lamplighters used long poles to reach the lights. This boy had a different method.*

*Tankers take on oil at the huge terminal on Kharg Island in the Persian Gulf. The island belongs to Iran, the fourth-largest oil producer in the world.*

# Drilling for oil

Oil and gas were created in a similar way to coal. But instead of coming from land plants, oil and gas formed from the remains of tiny animals and plants that lived in the world's oceans millions of years ago.

When these microscopic life-forms died, they sank to the seabed, where their remains were covered by mud and sand to form layers. Over a very long period of time, the remains were squashed and heated by the weight of more layers on top of them. This gradually turned the remains into oil, which also gave off bubbles of gas.

The layers of mud and sand, or sediments, turned into sandstone and other kinds of rock. The oil and gas flowed into holes in the surrounding rocks, until they were trapped by layers of completely solid, nonporous rocks. These pockets, or underground cavities, contain the fossil fuels that we drill for today.

*Some of the prehistoric seabed, where the oil layers originally formed, is now dry land. This tall oil derrick stands on the icy, frozen land of northern Russia.*

18

A rig in the North Sea, where more than 470 platforms produce oil and gas.

## Offshore rigs

Many oil and gas deposits are beneath the seabed. Engineers have had to work out ways of setting up derricks and drills directly above the deposits. In shallow water near the coast, fixed-leg rigs stand on the seabed. In deeper water, floating rigs have huge buoyancy tanks to keep them afloat and stable.

Both kinds of rigs have a large, flat platform for the framework of the derrick and other equipment. There is a landing pad for helicopters and living quarters for workers. Offshore rigs have to be strong to withstand stormy seas, but accidents have happened when rigs have collapsed or caught fire.

### HAZARDOUS CARGO

When an oil tanker has an accident and releases some or all of its cargo, enormous damage can be done to the environment by the oil. In 2002, a tanker called *Prestige* sank off the coast of Spain, causing a massive oil spill. The oil harmed many thousands of fish and seabirds, and polluted hundreds of miles of shoreline.

## Moving crude oil

Once a drill has struck a deposit, oil gushes to the surface. It is controlled by a series of valves before being pumped through pipelines to a storage tank. Some of the pipelines are very long (see pages 22–23). If the oil has to travel even farther to a refinery, perhaps on the other side of the world, it travels in enormous ships. Supertankers that can carry more than 330,000 tons (300,000 t) of oil are called ultra large crude carriers. The largest ships are more than 1,500 feet (450 m) long.

Clearing oil from a Spanish beach after the 2002 spill. The cleanup took many months.

# At the refinery

Crude oil, which is also called petroleum, is not used as a fuel in the form in which it comes out of the ground. It is processed and changed into many different kinds of oils and gases at a refinery.

Substances such as kerosene (which powers jet aircraft) and gasoline (which powers cars) are hydrocarbons. This means they are made up of different mixtures of the gas hydrogen and the element carbon. Hydrocarbon mixtures boil (and turn into a gas) and condense (and turn back into a liquid) at different temperatures. This makes it possible to separate the various substances in tall steel towers at the refinery. Heat, pressure, and chemicals are used in different processes to change one mixture of hydrocarbons into another.

*This oil refinery is at Grangemouth, in Scotland. The tall towers separate the substances. The steaming structures in the background are cooling towers. Refineries work 24 hours a day, shutting down only occasionally for maintenance.*

## Different oils and gases

At the refinery, crude oil is heated by a furnace to about 752 °F (400 °C). Then it passes into a tall column called a fractionating tower, where the oil is divided into different groups called fractions. The tower is hottest at the bottom and coolest at the top, and the substances with lower boiling points condense higher up. The heavier oils collect on trays near the bottom of the tower and flow out through pipes. Farther up the tower, lubricating oil, heating oil, kerosene, and then gasoline flow out. Some groups, such as butane, do not condense at all but stay as gases.

## Producing gasoline

Gasoline for motor fuel has been the most important product of the oil refining process since the early 20th century. Kerosene and diesel oil are also important fuels. Today, more than a third of the world's crude oil is refined into gasoline. We use so much as motor fuel that other processes are used in the refinery to change heavier fractions of oil into gasoline. Every day, we burn nearly 790 million gallons (3 billion l) of gasoline, more than two-fifths of this in the U.S.

*All of the processes in the tanks, pipes, and towers of the refinery are checked in a central control room.*

# The world of oil and gas

**A**ll of the world's continents have oil and gas, and these resources are under all of the world's oceans, too. The biggest producer of oil is Saudi Arabia.

Experts believe that the surrounding region of the Middle East holds about two-thirds of the world's oil reserves. The next largest producer is the U.S., which burns far more oil and gas than any other nation. Because of this, the U.S. has to import more than half of its oil.

Russia produces the most natural gas, followed by the U.S., Canada, and Britain. In Britain, the gas produced in the North Sea cannot meet the rising demand for gas that is caused by less coal production. So in the future, Britain will import gas from Norway through a 750-mile-long (1,200 km) underwater pipeline. Like other

*The Trans-Alaska pipeline runs for 800 miles (1,300 km) from oil fields in the north of Alaska to a port on the state's southern coast.*

*Offshore rigs like these in the Bay of Campeche produce a great deal of Mexico's oil.*

countries, Britain also wants to import liquefied natural gas (LNG). This is gas turned into a liquid by cooling it to a very low temperature. LNG takes up 600 times less space than the same amount of gas and is transported by ship in huge containers.

## Mexican oil

Oil was first discovered in Mexico in 1869 and was first produced commercially in 1901. Just 17 years later, Mexico was the second-biggest oil producer in the world, after the U.S. Shortly afterwards, the Mexican oil industry was supplying a quarter of the world's oil, and it exported most of it. Today, Mexico is the world's fifth-largest supplier, and it still produces more than twice the amount it uses. About three-quarters of its exports go to the U.S.

## Russian gas

Many of Russia's gas fields are in the frozen Siberian north, where the long winters are extremely cold. Russia produces more gas than it uses, so many long pipelines are being built. One will carry gas from Siberia to China and South Korea. Another is being built from offshore platforms in the Pacific Ocean near Sakhalin Island, which is a source of all three fossil fuels.

# Generating electricity

One of the most important uses of fossil fuels is for generating electricity. Together, coal, oil, and gas produce nearly two-thirds of the world's electrical power.

Coal is still the most popular energy source, and it generates more than three-quarters of the electricity used by countries such as Australia, China, and India. Before the coal is used, milling machines called pulverizers grind it into a fine powder. Hot air then blows the coal powder into a furnace, where it burns fiercely. This heats water in a boiler until it changes into steam, which

*The Kingston coal-fired power station in Tennessee has nine generators. It uses about 14,300 tons (13,000 t) of coal every day to produce electricity for more than 700,000 homes.*

drives an electric generator. A large power station uses several million tons of bituminous coal every year.

Oil-fired and gas-fired power plants work in the same way. The oil or gas is burned in a combustion chamber, creating the heat needed to boil water and produce steam.

## Turbines and generators

Inside a power station, turbines and generators change mechanical energy into electrical energy. The mechanical energy is the power of high-pressure steam, created by burning fossil fuels. The steam turns the blades of a turbine, which is connected by a shaft to a generator.

Inside the generator, the shaft makes magnets spin inside wire coils to produce electricity. This technology was first used in 1831, when British scientist Michael Faraday discovered that he could create electricity by moving a magnet through a coil of copper wire. The basic idea is still the same today.

## Transmitting power

Power stations are generally built close to their energy source, such as a coal mine, fuel terminal, or oil refinery. Devices called transformers make the electricity produced by the plant's generators more powerful. This makes it easier to transmit the electric current long distances along cables.

The power lines are carried on tall pylons to towns and cities, where another set of transformers changes the current back to a lower voltage (or power). Then the electricity is sent to individual homes and businesses.

*These engineers are working on the shaft attached to the wheel of a power plant turbine.*

# Environmental problems

Using fossil fuels as energy sources creates great problems. One is that the processes of removing them from the earth, by mining and drilling, damage the environment.

Transporting fuels, especially oil, can also lead to environmental damage. There have been many disastrous oil spills, especially from tankers, that have polluted long stretches of coastline. But the greatest problem with fossil fuels is that they pollute the air when they are burned.

Fumes from power stations and car engines, including the gases sulfur and nitrogen, drift high in the air and dissolve in the water droplets of clouds. This makes acid rain, which damages rivers, lakes, and forests when it falls on them. Burning fossil fuels also produces carbon dioxide, which is known as a greenhouse gas. Carbon dioxide in the air helps to soak up and trap heat from the sun. As the world demand for energy increases, these problems will also increase if we continue to use fossil fuels.

*Acid rain has damaged these trees in a German forest.*

## Landscape at risk

In 2005, the U.S. government gave the go-ahead for oil exploration on the coastal plain of northern Alaska near the village of Kaktovic. This is less than 125 miles (200 km) from the oil fields near Prudhoe Bay, which have been worked since 1968. The difference is that the new region lies within the Arctic National Wildlife Refuge. This is an area where wild animals and their habitat should be protected. Opponents of the new oil field fear that it will damage the environment and threaten wildlife. If we continue to search for new sources of fossil fuels, the world's last wildernesses will disappear.

*Caribou cross a river in the Alaska National Wildlife Refuge. They may be endangered by oil exploration, along with musk oxen, polar bears, grizzly bears, snow geese, and many other animals.*

*This photograph shows air pollution in Mexico City. This is mainly caused by exhaust fumes from the millions of cars that people drive in the city.*

### CLIMATE CHANGE

Releasing too much carbon dioxide and other gases into the air leads to a greenhouse effect, trapping heat. Scientists believe that this has caused temperatures to rise slightly around the world. They call this global warming and believe that it is causing ice to melt in the polar regions. This could lead to a rise in sea levels around the world and cause the flooding of coastal areas.

# Future trends

Scientists have been searching for new energy sources for many years. They have discovered oil shale, a rock that contains a form of crude oil. This can be released by heating the rock, but the process uses a lot of energy.

Another possible energy source is the methane gas contained in rock crystals beneath the seabed. But this might be dangerous to mine and would have all of the disadvantages of other fossil fuels when burned.

Engineers are working on new power sources for cars, using hydrogen gas and other substances to drive fuel cells and produce electricity. Some of these ideas may work in the future, and further possibilities will be discovered. But most experts believe that the best way forward is to use renewable resources. At the same time, we must look for ways to conserve energy by using it as efficiently as possible.

*Manufacturers are looking for new ways to power cars. This model uses hydrogen.*

## RENEWABLE ALTERNATIVES

The future of fossil fuels as energy sources is in doubt. Many countries are looking more seriously than ever at renewable sources, such as wind, water, solar, and biomass power. These sources won't run out, and they are greener, or cleaner, than fossil fuels. They have less impact on the environment, and they do not pollute the air. However, there is still a great deal of work to be done to make sure that these alternatives can provide all of the energy the world needs.

*Most of Greenland is covered by a thick ice sheet. Scientists warn that the ice will melt into the sea more quickly if global warming continues. Reducing carbon dioxide could help prevent this.*

## International agreements

In recent years, international agreements have aimed to reduce the amounts of greenhouse gases that countries release. Some countries have agreed to targets, but not all have signed agreements. In 2005, the European Union started its own program, and more than 15,000 power stations, refineries, and factories were told how much carbon dioxide they could emit. If they go over the limit, they have to pay fines or buy allowances from others who have beaten their targets. Such programs could become much more widespread in the future.

*The future may lie with small-scale solar panels and wind turbines.*

# Glossary

**anthracite**  A very black, glossy kind of hard coal; the oldest form of coal.

**archaeologist**  A person who studies the ancient past by digging up and looking at remains.

**bituminous coal**  A kind of soft coal that burns with a smoky flame.

**brine**  Salty water.

**charcoal**  A black form of carbon made by heating wood.

**coke**  A solid fuel made from coal.

**condense**  To change from a gas into a liquid.

**crude oil**  Oil as it is found naturally underground.

**derrick**  A framework that supports drilling equipment.

**diesel (or diesel oil)**  A fuel obtained from crude oil that is similar to gasoline.

**environmentalist**  A person who is concerned about and acts to protect the natural environment.

**fossil fuel**  A fuel (such as coal, oil, and natural gas) that comes from the remains of prehistoric plants and animals.

**fractionating tower**  A tall column in which crude oil is separated into different substances.

**furnace**  An oven-like structure in which materials can be heated to very high temperatures.

**generator**  A machine that turns mechanical energy into electrical energy.

**geologist**  A scientist who studies Earth's structure.

**global warming**  The heating up of Earth's surface, especially caused by pollution from burning fossil fuels.

**greenhouse effect** The warming of Earth's surface (called global warming) caused especially by pollution from burning fossil fuels.

**greenhouse gas** A gas, such as carbon dioxide, that traps heat from the sun near Earth and helps to create the greenhouse effect.

**hydrocarbon** A chemical compound containing hydrogen and carbon.

**Industrial Revolution** The rapid development of machinery, factories, and industry that began in the late 18th century.

**kiln** An oven used for firing, or baking, clay pots.

**lignite** A soft, crumbly kind of brown coal; the youngest form of coal.

**liquefied natural gas (LNG)** Natural gas in the form of a liquid.

**nonrenewable resources** Resources that are used up and cannot be replaced.

**offshore** In the sea not far from the coast.

**oil field** An area where there are large reserves of oil that can be extracted.

**ore** A rock or mineral containing a useful metal or valuable mineral.

**peat** A spongy, wet mass of decomposed vegetation that is the first stage in the formation of coal.

**petroleum** Crude oil.

**piston** A cylinder that is pushed up and down inside an engine.

**pocket** An underground cavity where oil and/or gas are trapped.

**pollute** To damage with harmful substances.

**power station** A plant where electricity is generated.

**pylon** A tall, metal tower that supports power cables.

**refinery** An industrial plant where oil and gas are processed and purified.

**reserves** Supplies that have not yet been used.

**seam** A layer of coal between layers of other rocks.

**smelt** To heat and melt ore in order to get metal from it.

**strip mine** A mine in which ore is extracted at or near the surface of the earth.

**transformer** A device that changes the power of an electric current.

**turbine** A machine with rotating blades.

**voltage** Electric power expressed in units called volts.

# Index